AEC SINGLE-DECKERS

HOWARD BERRY

AMBERLEY

First published 2018

Amberley Publishing
The Hill, Stroud
Gloucestershire, GL5 4EP

www.amberley-books.com

Copyright © Howard Berry, 2018

The right of Howard Berry to be identified as
the Author of this work has been asserted in
accordance with the Copyrights, Designs and
Patents Act 1988.

ISBN 978 1 4456 7672 2 (print)
ISBN 978 1 4456 7673 9 (ebook)

British Library Cataloguing in Publication Data.
A catalogue record for this book is available from
the British Library.

Origination by Amberley Publishing.
Printed in the UK.

Introduction

The Associate Equipment Company (AEC) was one of the leaders in British commercial and passenger vehicle manufacturing. In 1908, the London General and London Motor Omnibus Companies merged to form the London General Omnibus Company (LGOC). In 1912, the LGOC was taken over by the Underground Electric Railways of London, and the vehicle building activities were separated off to form AEC. In 1927, the famous Southall factory in West London produced its first vehicles, and until closure in 1979, AEC produced some of the finest buses and coaches made by a British manufacturer. While not everything AEC built was a success, their overriding popularity was down to their products being reliable, steady performers, with one of the most melodious engine notes of all time. Such was the loyalty to AEC that when the end of passenger chassis production was announced, a group of major coach operators persuaded the Leyland Group, the then owners of AEC, to re-engineer the Leyland Leopard to meet their requirements. Others felt that Leyland couldn't match the quality of the vehicles they had been used to, and switched their allegiance to foreign chassis such as Volvo and DAF.

In 1984, five years after the last chassis rolled off the production line, Brian Goulding led a group of likeminded enthusiasts to form the AEC Society, with the aim of documenting, preserving and appreciating the products of AEC. The society has grown to be one of the largest single-make heavy vehicle clubs in the country; members include preservationists and operators of AECs both at home and abroad, as well as former employees, drivers and mechanics. Many members are enthusiasts who have happy memories of AECs operating in their own locality, or who took an interest in a particular haulage or passenger fleet. With so many vehicles produced by AEC, it is impossible to do them justice in just one book, and this volume, produced in association with the AEC Society, showcases single-deck PSVs starting with the Regal IV, through to probably the finest British-built coach to grace the roads – the Reliance. I apologise now if there are any inaccuracies contained within, as while the official information on the history of each chassis is cast in stone, the comments for the photographs might not be as sharp as the photographs themselves – remember, it is now almost forty years since the last AECs rolled out of Southall. Joking aside, I wish to give a huge thank you to the following photographers who have allowed me to use their work, and to whom an initialled credit is given after each photograph: Alan Snatt (AS), Cliff Essex (CE), Martyn Hearson (MH), Martin Perry (MP), Norman Chambers (NC), Neil Gow (NG), Richard Cripps (RC), Richard Simons (RS), Steve Guess (SG), Ray Jones (RJ), and Terry Walker (TW).

I hope that you find this, my first attempt at a mainstream publication, to be informative, interesting and, above all, as enjoyable to read as it was to write.

The Regal IV and VI

In 1939, AEC experimented with an underfloor-engined chassis intended for the Canadian market. Fitted with AEC's new 9.6 litre engine placed amidships between the axles and fitted with a Park Royal body, the outbreak of the Second World War put an end to this experiment. However, the lessons learned gave AEC ample experience when it came to the design and production of their first mainstream underfloor-engined vehicle – the Regal IV. Prior to its introduction, PSV chassis tended to be to a half cab design, with the engine adjacent to the driver. Not only did this leave the driver isolated from the passengers, but it also meant that stage carriage operations required a conductor, adding to the operating costs of the vehicle. The Regal IV was to change all this – the engine was redesigned to fit horizontally between the axles, allowing the passenger door to be located opposite the driver and designed to take bodywork up to the maximum length of 27 feet 6 inches. A prototype was built in 1949, feedback from which convinced AEC to put the Regal IV into production, but before this could be done the maximum length of single-deck PSV's was increased to 30 feet, and AEC were quick to take advantage of this, with only the prototype and twenty-five vehicles already ordered by London Transport having been built to the original length. London Transport were to be the largest operator of the Regal IV, operating 700 examples in the RF class, which were built to a width of 7 feet 6 inches and incorporating several mechanical features common only to LT buses.

Despite cost-savings exercises made with the introduction of driver-only buses, operators still had to keep a close eye on finances – wages were rising, and signs of a fall in passenger numbers were being seen, mainly due to the increase in private car ownership. Operators were paying close attention to fuel costs, and the Regal IV was quite a heavy vehicle, its fuel consumption being higher than comparative models from other manufacturers, and this undoubtedly explained why it never achieved popularity as a service bus with operators outside London as it did within. It did, however, find favour as a coach chassis, with high-profile operators such as Yelloway, Wallace Arnold, and the Scottish Bus Group standardising on it for their coaching requirements. Altogether, over 2,600 Regal IVs were built and while production finished for the UK market in 1955, it remained available for export until the mid-1960s.

At the 1960 Commercial Motor Show, AEC announced an updated version of the Regal IV intended purely as an export model. Designated Regal VI, and fitted with the 11.3 litre AH690 engine, it was available in both left- and right-hand variants, two different wheelbases and options such as air suspension and power steering. The largest orders came from South America, with Buenos Aires ordering 500, and 150 vehicles delivered to Montevideo, Uruguay.

The start of it all: UMP 277, the prototype Park Royal-bodied Regal IV, entered service with London Transport at St Albans in 1950. After evaluation by provincial operators, it returned to AEC to act as internal staff transport, receiving AEC's factory livery of yellow and blue. Acquired for preservation in 1971, its full restoration was completed in 2013. (SG)

Hampton Court Green sees 1953 Harrington-bodied Regal IV PYB 240 in the livery of Blackwell, Earls Colne, Essex. New to Bowerman of Taunton, then passing to Greenslades of Exeter, the coach was actually owned by fellow Essex operator Hedingham & District, who had acquired the Blackwell business in 1966. (RC)

Fitted with 8-foot-wide ECW bodywork with glass roof panels and opening roof, the fifteen members of London Transport's RFW class of touring coaches were unlike anything seen before in the LT fleet. Now preserved, RFW 14 (LUC 389) is seen in Sutton Town Centre in 1980. (SG)

Ripponden & District was synonymous with parcel deliveries until the early part of this century, but its origins were in passenger transport, purchasing Whitson-bodied Regal IV LWT 149 new in 1952. It passed two years later to fellow Yorkshire operator Marshall of Bradford, and is seen in 1965 at Hampton Court Green with the driver rooting through his loose change to pay the parking fee. (RC)

Willowbrook-bodied Regal IV TCR 683 (NUO 683) was new in 1953 to Devon General and was allocated to the Grey Cars fleet. It is seen here on less luxurious work parked in Colchester bus station while on a private hire, now in the immaculate fleet of Vines (yes, that is without an apostrophe) of Great Bromley. (RC)

The Scottish registration and Alexander bodywork give away former Western SMT HWS 940's origins. New in 1951, it was fitted with a toilet for use on London services. It is seen here in Colchester bus station with Vines operating a duplicate holiday express service to the East Midlands. (RC)

Cheddleton, on the Churnet Valley Railway, with a Mk1 Ford Capri and austerity saddle tank flanking Plaxton-bodied Regal IV RMB 240 from the fleet of Bassett of Tittensor. Bassett's were renowned for getting long working lives from their fleet of coaches and lorries, and RMB 240, new in 1953 to Altrincham Coachways, lasted in the fleet until the early 1980s. (MH)

Bassett of Tittensor again, this time with Gurney Nutting-bodied Regal IV PEH 600, which was new to local operator Need of Longton. This 1973 view taken in the depot sees it in the company of 5002 NC, a Duple Yeoman-bodied Thames Trader. The Trader was new to Spencer of Manchester, who merged with Smith of Wigan, who in turn merged with Happiway of Manchester to form another prolific AEC operator – Smiths Happiway-Spencer. (TW)

Ipswich were long-standing AEC users, with large fleets of Regals, Regents and Swifts. BPV 8 was one of a batch of six Park Royal forty-two-seat Regal IVs delivered in 1953. In 1967, it was down-seated to forty seats and converted to driver-only operation. Sold for preservation in 1973, it is seen here in 1977 far from its original home, crossing the Woolwich ferry. (SG)

September 1952 saw East Yorkshire independent Everingham Brothers of Pocklington take delivery of KWF 761 and KWF 762, two Regal IVs bodied by locally based Barnaby of Hull. Shortly after delivery, Everingham's were taken over by East Yorkshire Motor Services, where the Regals lasted until 1965. This 1963 shot shows the pair leaving Doncaster Racecourse on St Leger Day. (RS)

City of Oxford purchased nearly 450 AECs before becoming a member of the National Bus Company. Their first Regal IVs were ten Willowbrook-bodied examples delivered in 1952, consisting of four coaches and six buses. One of the latter is seen in 1966, parked on Angel Hill in Bury St Edmunds after purchase by Theobald of Long Melford, Suffolk. (RC)

Barton of Chilwell had a varied vehicle-buying policy, even rebuilding vehicles to their own specifications. In 1966, Barton acquired Provincial Coaches of Leicester, with Plaxton Venturer-bodied Regal IV HJF 61 being the oldest vehicle retained by Barton. It is seen in 1970 in Huntingdon Street bus station, Nottingham. (TW)

The classic lines of Burlingham's Seagull are seen here on JCY 870, which was new in 1952 to Welsh independent Evans of Llangennech. Over twenty years later it had made its way to the north of the country and is seen here in 1973 with Caernarfon-based Penygroes Coaches. (TW)

After ending their operational lives, many buses and coaches pass into non-PSV use. One such vehicle was Willowbrook-bodied NUO 684, new in 1953 to the Grey Cars division of Devon General. By 1977, it had passed to Ninestones Riding School in Bolventor, Cornwall, and was still looking good despite being nearly twenty-five years old. (TW)

New in 1952 to Mulley's Motorways of Ixworth, Sussex, Burlingham-bodied Regal IV 7227 TU was originally registered ECF 111. Jack Mulley was renowned for keeping withdrawn vehicles and in 1975 there were so many that a disposal sale was held. ECF 111 was sold for the princely sum of £125 to Cheshire haulier Edwin C. Farrell, who bought it for the registration rather than the coach. Preserved in Mulley's livery, the coach currently resides in Holland. (SG)

Ipswich again; this time 1971 and with examples of nearly every type of AEC operated by the Corporation at the time. Regal IV BPV 12 is seen in Prince's Street, sandwiched between an unidentified Swift and Regent V DPV 66D with a fine array of cars in the background. (AS)

Formed in the early 1930s by a group of Cambridge undergraduates as a diversion to their studies, the two-tone blue of Premier Travel became a familiar sight up and down the country. As well as a network of local services around East Anglia, long-distance express services were also operated. Until the 1980s, the fleet completely comprised British-built vehicles, including Burlingham Seagull-bodied Regal IV 123 (XMT55), seen here in Haverhill. (RC)

The sixty-five Park Royal-bodied Regal IVs delivered to London Transport to undertake the BEA airport transfer contract appear to have been very camera-shy when in service, but luckily a number still exist in varying conditions of repair. MLL 738 is seen here in preservation, the BEA badge prominently displayed on the front in place of the AEC triangle or LT roundel. (SG)

By the late 1970s, MLL 725 had taken up residence in Longport Canal Wharf, Stoke-on-Trent, where it was being used as a mobile portrait studio by Colorama Portraits of London. It was oddly also carrying lettering for AAFES, the American Army & Air Force Exchange Service. (MH)

By the early 1980s, MLL 725 had given up its life of art and moved to the Leicestershire village of Sileby for a new role as a mobile caravan (although looking at the number of items placed around the windows, movement seems highly unlikely). I assume that the rope on the nearside front corner was a washing line rather than a guy rope to prevent it being blown away! After passing to two further owners in the same area for similar use, it was scrapped in 1985. (TW)

Looking decidedly better cared for is MLL 754, which is seen parked on Trent Bridge, Nottingham, in 1969, acting as tour bus for a band called Peppermint Circus. (TW)

Eastbourne coach park in 1977 shows what at first glance looks like a Bristol MW. LYM 730 was in fact one of five Regal IVs delivered to Tilling's of London in 1951, fitted with ECW coach bodies similar to the LT RFW class. In 1960 they were returned to ECW, where they received bodies identical to those being fitted to the MW. After sale, all five ended up with Denyer Brothers of Stondon Massey, where they remained until the early 2000s, when all were rescued. (AS)

The Ambassador, perhaps not the prettiest body Duple ever produced, is seen here on LTX 470, one of three Regal IVs delivered to Brewer of Caerau in 1952. It is seen here in Swansea in 1969, still looking smart for a seventeen-year-old coach. (AS)

In 1952, Lancaster City Transport acquired four Burlingham-bodied Regal IVs from Rochdale Corporation. The buses were only four years old at the time and were part of a larger batch, the rest of which remained with Rochdale until 1968. Looking immaculate for a seventeen-year-old bus, JDK 714 is seen in Lancaster bus station in 1969. (AS)

With accident damage to the front nearside corner and in need of a good clean, RF452 (MXX 429) is seen at Weybridge in January 1978. (SG)

You would like to think that the female passenger is giving admiring glances to RFs 489/528 and 521 (MXX 456, MLL 946 and MXX 489) as they bask in the autumn sunshine inside the old Kingston bus station, waiting to depart on service in 1976. (AS)

The restricted size of the inspection pits at Kingston Garage gave the RFs allocated there for routes 218 and 219 a stay of execution, as suitable replacement vehicles could not be found. The problem was solved by moving the routes to Norwood Garage, and on 30 March 1979, the last day of operation, RFs 526 and 528, together with two others, sit in the garage awaiting their fate. (SG)

In the mid-1960s, LT's image consultants decided that the Greenline RFs needed a makeover. Externally, the waistbands received aluminium beading, the headlights were replaced with dual clusters, and, as can be seen here, the roof boards were painted yellow. RF93 (LYF 444) rounds Parliament Square, Westminster, en route to High Wycombe in 1972. (AS)

The modernisation plan also included the removal of the LT bullseye from the radiator filler cap, which in some cases was overpainted with a non-matching shade of green, as seen here on RF70, which is photographed in London Road, Dorking, in August 1973. (RC)

Modernised RFs demoted from Greenline work received a canary yellow band, as shown on RF183 (MLL 570). The bus is seen in Clarence Street in Kingston, on Green Line route 718 to Windsor, after all the green RFs had been transferred to the newly formed London Country Bus Services. (RC)

Its roof lights identifying it as one of the original twenty-five RFs ordered just before the maximum length for PSVs increased to 30 feet, is LUC 212, formerly RF12. This vehicle, together with sister RF13, saw further service in Shropshire with Hampson of Oswestry. Lasting into the 1980s on the Oswestry town service, it is seen here in the depot in the company of two newer members of the fleet. (MH)

Blue Saloon of Guildford used six RFs on local work, the last of which was NLE 679 (former RF679), which remained until the mid-1980s. It is being followed through Guildford by another 'last', JTM 109V, which was the last Duple-bus-bodied Reliance to be built. (MH)

The private hire RFs proved to be popular second-hand buys, with former RF10 passing to Osbornes of Tollesbury. Immaculately presented in this 1965 shot taken in Colchester bus station in the company of ONO 177 is a Bedford OB of Went of Boxted. (RC)

Carmarthenshire independent Eynon of Trimsaran operated a varied fleet until its sad demise in the 1980s. Two RFs were purchased: MLL 934 (RF516) lasted all of two months, but the second example, MXX 489 (RF512), fared much better, remaining in service until 1985. Seen here after withdrawal in what can only be described as semi-derelict condition, it was happily saved for preservation. (MH)

The Cambridge-based Traffic Research Centre purchased four RFs from LT, which all ended their lives as store sheds on an Army base. Approximately ten years ago they were required to leave the base, and, despite their looks, were driven to their new home, one even passing an MOT a few days later! (MH)

Sadly not a member of the author's 'fantasy fleet': after sale by LT in 1976, former RF371 (MXX 13) started a new life as staff transport for Howard Rotavators, Halesworth, and is seen here in the company of former Eastern Counties ECW-bodied Bristol SC 6569 NG. (TW)

Guildford town centre again with former RF389 (MXX 277), showing how Blue Saloon took advantage of the large destination screen to give full route information. This vehicle was originally purchased from LT by the London Bus Preservation Group in October 1976, passing to Blue Saloon a month later. (TW)

Let's hope the Traffic Warden didn't find any issues with the parking of ex-London Country RFs 657/605 and 60, seen here outside Heathrow Terminal 1. Having passed to Halls/Silverline Coaches of Hounslow, all three were used on airside transfer work. (AS)

AECs exported to certain overseas countries were badged as ACLO due to fears of trademark infringement by the German electrical giant AEG. The Regal VI was developed specifically for the overseas market, and a joint venture with Dutch bodybuilder Verheul saw over 150 vehicles produced for the South American market. (AEC)

During the Second World War the Belgian railway system was decimated, forcing NMBS, the state-owned railway company, to introduce permanently contracted bus services. The De Deene family of Ghent successfully obtained a number of contracts for their Diana Cars fleet. In 1963, still operating on behalf of NMBS, Diana Cars took delivery of six Jonckheere-bodied Regal VIs, one of which is seen in Ghent on the fast service to Antwerp. (RC)

The Swift and Sabre

While the move towards underfloor engine single-deck vehicles for coaching operations had been underway for some years, bus services were traditionally operated by double-deck vehicles crewed by a driver and conductor. By the early 1960s, legislation changes allowed driver-only operation on single-deck buses, and deliveries of such vehicles gained ground across the country. While attractive to operators who could now almost halve their labour costs, passengers found the step heights required to enter underfloor-engined buses cumbersome, leading to delays while boarding and alighting. In order to lower the floor height, manufacturers renewed their interest in producing rear-engined single-deck buses, with Bristol producing their successful RE model in 1962. The Leyland Motor Corporation, which by now included AEC, reacted with a range of vehicles based on a standardised frame and steering layout, leaving individual manufacturers to source their own engines and gearboxes. AEC's offering, announced in 1964, was 36 feet long, had the new 8.2 litre AH505 engine, monocontrol (semi-automatic) transmission and was called the Swift. It was also available with a six-speed constant mesh gearbox and high floor suitable for coach operations. AEC announced that there would be a heavier duty version fitted with the 11.3 litre AH691 engine and this model would be called the Merlin; however, the name was never officially adopted and the models became known as the Swift 505 and Swift 691. Operators were keen to try the new Swifts, and following requests for a shorter length version, a 33-foot 6-inch-version was introduced; however, the shorter rear overhang was not long enough for the AH691 engine, so all short Swifts were fitted with the smaller AH505 engine. At the same time, the coach version was withdrawn for the home market.

One of the first operators to order the Swift was London Transport, and having taken delivery of fifteen full-length Swift AH691s would eventually operate 665 examples on the streets of London, and in a nod to the original AEC type name, referred to these vehicles as 'Merlins'. Bodywork on the original fifteen was by Strachan, with the balance supplied by Metro-Cammell, and were designated MB (single or dual door), MBS (dual door), and MBA (dual door with turnstile payment system and large standee area for use on Red Arrow services). Sadly, the Merlin wasn't the hoped-for success; Union negotiations over one-person operation and extended driver training times delayed them entering service and meant hardly any operational experience had been gained before the final vehicles were delivered. Almost immediately it was found that there was great difficulty manoeuvring a 36-foot bus in London, and while the Strachan-bodied examples were well built, Metro-Cammell failed to appreciate the stresses having the engine suspended at the rear placed on the body and chassis, leading to an urgent rectification programme after holes started to appear along the roofline. Overheating was also common, caused mainly by a hard-working engine and frequent stops, as when the engine idled, so did the cooling fan. LT ordered no more Merlins, and instead switched to the 10-metre Swift, with delivery of nearly 840 commencing in 1969, bodied this time by Marshall and Park Royal. The shorter Swifts were also troublesome, with the 8.3 litre engine being considered to be underpowered and leading to engine failures. The first Merlins were withdrawn in 1973, and the majority were out of service by 1975. Withdrawals of the Swifts started in 1976, and by 1979 over half the class had been withdrawn. This meant that there were hundreds of relatively new, well maintained buses available to the open market. While many were scrapped, others went on to have second lives at home and abroad, with large batches being exported to Malta and Australia.

Outside London, Swifts sold in large batches to municipal operators such as St Helens, Great Yarmouth, Blackpool, Leeds, Sheffield and Aberdeen. Some operators got long service lives from their Swifts – Blackpool and Great Yarmouth, with both operating Swifts until the late 1980s/early 1990s. For other operators, Swifts were not considered a success, and in certain terrains overheating was a common problem. Following withdrawal from service with their original operators, many were sold on for further use. Staffordshire-based independent Knotty Bus ran a fleet of four Swifts between 1988 and 1995, and despite operating an intensive service across the hilly Potteries, found them to be reliable and rugged machines. Swifts also sold well on the export market, with the antipodes especially fond of them, where Australian Capital Territory operator ACTION purchased 101 AH505-powered Swifts between 1967 and 1975, while the State Transport Authority of Adelaide purchased 292 AH691-powered Swifts in 1970–72, followed by sixty-six AH760 examples in 1978. While the coach version of the Swift failed to take off in the home market, it was a different matter in Portugal, where Lisbon coachbuilder UTIC built rear-engined integral vehicles using AEC Swift components and ZF gearboxes. They proved popular and the last examples delivered to the state-owned Rodovaria Nacional were only withdrawn in 2009.

One final rear-engined AEC which must be mentioned is the Sabre. The Sabre VP2R was powered by AEC's 247 bhp V8 engine coupled to a five-speed semi-automatic gearbox. Four chassis were built, two with left-hand drive, which were exported to Portugal and Israel, and two right-hand drive chassis, one of which was exported to Australia and bodied locally by Denning. The fourth chassis remained in the UK, where it was fitted with a forty-six-seat ECW coach body. The V8 was probably AEC's least successful engine (lack of sufficient development time being cited as the main reason), and CBU 636J was to remain unique. Still around today, but not in operational status, we can only hope that this historically important vehicle is restored one day.

Two Swift demonstrators were built: Willowbrook-bodied FGW 498C and Marshall-bodied LYY 827D. In this official AEC photograph, the latter is seen outside one of the large hangars at Marshall's Cambridge premises. It was subsequently sold to Ulsterbus and registered CIA 3000. (AEC)

Following the success of a lone Swift ordered to test the practicality of operating 36-foot buses over city routes, Southampton took delivery of a further nine in 1968/9. The first batch of five were fitted with locally built Strachan Pacemaker bodies, outwardly similar to the first batch of Merlins delivered to London Transport. Freshly withdrawn number 6 (MTR 424F) looks remarkably tidy in this 1980 photograph, though closer examination shows damage to both nearside corners. (MH)

Ipswich bought eleven Swifts: six Willowbrook-bodied examples followed by a batch of five with East Lancs. Ornately numbered 91 (DDX 91L) is seen at Electric House, the Ipswich town centre terminus in 1974. (AS)

Very few independent operators purchased Swifts; however, one operator who made a repeat order was Red Rover of Aylesbury, ordering two for their intensive network of town services around Buckinghamshire. By early 1980, EPP 59G had passed to Warwickshire operator Catterall of Southam, and is seen at their depot flanked by two Harrington Grenadier-bodied Reliances. (MH)

Waveney District Council was possibly the shortest lived municipal operator. Formed under the 1974 Local Government Reorganisation to take over the operations of Lowestoft Council, operations ceased less than four years later, the vehicles passed to neighbouring Great Yarmouth Borough Transport. The last vehicles bought were two Swifts fitted with Lowestoft-built ECW bodies; the second, 18 (NRT 565L), is seen here in Lowestoft in 1977. (SG)

Tucked away in south Suffolk is the village of Boxford, which was once home to Rule's Coaches. For many years the fleet consisted mainly of AECs, most of which gave many years' service. Seen at their yard is GRT 865J, one of the earlier batch of Lowestoft Swifts. Rule's closed their doors in the early part of this century; however, their name lives on, as the land where the depot stood was sold for housing and is now called Rule's Yard. (RJ)

As well as acquiring the ex-Lowestoft/Waveney Swifts, Great Yarmouth had a sizeable Swift fleet of its own. They were to have long lives by the seaside, lasting well into the 1990s, and the author remembers one being a regular performer on the Great Yarmouth to King's Lynn College run – a journey of over 90 miles on a twenty-plus-year-old service bus. One of the last survivors was WEX 687M, fitted with the later style of ECW bodywork. (MH)

The deregulation of the British bus industry in 1986 allowed easier opportunity for competition on local bus services, usually against the established operators. Citybus of Chadderton began operating a network of services across north Manchester against the incumbent GM Buses. They ran a collection of Swifts, Leyland Panthers and Bristol REs, among other exotic machines. LEX 865H, an ex-Yarmouth Willowbrook-bodied Swift, is seen here crossing Piccadilly Gardens, Manchester. (MH)

Municipal operators tended to purchase bodywork from their local coachbuilders, with Leeds City Transport favouring the products of Crossgates-based Charles. H. Roe for the near 600 AECs operated. Leeds was also one of the largest Swift operators, with one being the last AEC delivered before Leeds was merged into West Yorkshire PTE. In a break from the norm, fifty Park Royal-bodied Swifts were delivered in 1969, including 1003 (SUB 403G), which is seen in Leeds Central bus station in 1971. (AS)

Only the fleet number gives away the fact that Roe-bodied Swift MVH 27F had passed into the ownership of West Yorkshire PTE. Formerly Huddersfield Corporation 27, it retained the municipality's livery when photographed in its home town. Note how the traditional Huddersfield livery has been amended to outline the AEC winged triangle badge. (RS)

Bradford City Transport operated Britain's last commercial trolleybus system. The withdrawal of the trolleybuses commenced in 1962 when ten AEC Regents Vs were purchased in readiness for trolleybus conversion, yet it was 1972 – a further ten years later – before the last trolleybuses were withdrawn. Two years on, Bradford City Transport itself was no more, having been swallowed up by West Yorkshire PTE. The last AECs to enter the fleet were five Marshall-bodied Swifts, including 503 (NAK 503H), seen when new in Bridge Street, Bradford, with the trolleybus wires still much in evidence. (AS)

Better known for their coach touring operations, Wallace Arnold of Leeds had a small stage carriage operation based on the former Hardwick's service from Scarborough to Allerston. In 1971, to facilitate driver-only operation, four three-year-old ex-Sheffield Swifts were purchased. Unfortunately, they proved to be unreliable (when the four were collected, one even refused to start, so a replacement was taken) and were sold after three years. (RS)

Blackpool ordered fifty-five Swifts between 1969 and 1974. All were bodied by Marshall, with the first ten having semi-automatic gearboxes. The remainder were fitted with fully auto units. The first withdrawals started in 1980 when they were only ten years old, but the survivors soldiered on until 1988. Seen turning into Talbot Square opposite Blackpool's famous North Pier is 550 (PFR 550H), displaying the rather rudimentary heavy-duty bumper fitted to this batch. (AS)

OFR 983M was one of Blackpool's last Swifts, and saw further service with enthusiastic Staffordshire operator Knotty Bus of Newcastle-under-Lyme. Seen here lettered up to celebrate Knotty's fifth anniversary, it was destroyed by fire at the company's premises in the late 1990s. (MH)

W. R. and P. Bingley of Kinsley in South Yorkshire, together with fellow independents Cooper of South Elmsall and Everett of South Kirby, traded as United Services, operating between Wakefield and Doncaster. The last new bus bought by Bingley was Willowbrook-bodied Swift SWT 704F, seen here leaving Doncaster bus station. (RS)

After sale by Bingley, SWT 704F passed to one of Staffordshire's more interesting operators, Stonier of Goldenhill. Looking decidedly battle scarred, it is seen departing Hanley bus station en route to Meir. (RS)

With Sheffield's imposing Park Hill housing estate looming in the misty background, Sheffield JOC's Park Royal-bodied 1020 (TWE 120F) turns into Pond Street bus station in 1969. Sheffield's bus fleet was actually three fleets in one: the 'A' fleet owned entirely by the corporation and operated within the city boundary, the 'B' fleet owned jointly by the Corporation and the British Railways Board, operating in the outer suburbs, and the 'C' fleet, owned entirely by the BRB, ran to such exotic destinations as Manchester, Buxton and Chesterfield. (AS)

West Bridgford UDC operated a sizable fleet of AEC Regents, but declining passenger numbers led to three Swifts (to be registered KRR 243–5E) being ordered for delivery in 1967. Intended for driver-only operation, Trades Union pressure prevented this from taking place, and before they were delivered West Bridgford sold out to neighbouring Nottingham City Transport. All three were delivered directly to NCT and were registered NAL 543–5F. The middle of the three is seen on its original home territory, travelling through West Bridgford. (RC)

St Helens ordered sixty-three Swifts over a ten-year period, all of which were bodied by Marshall. Seen in Victoria Square, St Helens, shortly after delivery, while still wearing its rear wheel covers and displaying the corporation crest on its vibrant red livery, is 224 (TDJ 224G). (AS)

St Helens again, but now firmly in the Merseyside PTE era, is 230 (TDG 230G). Disappearing off behind is a Leyland National – the vehicle that effectively killed off both the Swift and Bristol RE for the home market. (MH)

The 'DK' registration mark will always be associated with Rochdale, whether on one of the Corporation's fleet of AECs, or one of the orange and yellow Reliances of well-respected and much missed coaching firm Yelloway. While Rochdale did have some Swifts, by the time Pennine-bodied TDK 548J had been delivered Rochdale had become part of SELNEC – the PTE formed to serve South-East Lancashire and North-East Cheshire. In this 1977 view in Leigh, SELNEC had now become Greater Manchester PTE. (AS)

Mention was made earlier of Stonier of Goldenhill. In 1976, the company was sold to fellow Staffordshire operator Berresford's of Cheddleton, becoming a stand-alone subsidiary of the Berresford Group. This is how it continued until 1987, when, following the death of Jim Berresford, the group was purchased by the newly privatised PMT. Out of the ten swifts diverted from Rochdale to SELNEC, Berresford's purchased eight. Seen in 1981 at the back of Goldenhill depot is the newly acquired and freshly painted TDK 541J. (MH)

Sunderland Corporation took Strachan bodywork on their Swifts, taking ten in 1968. Sunderland was another operator to become a constituent of a transport authority, becoming part of Tyneside PTA in 1973, with Tyneside subsequently becoming Tyne & Wear PTE in 1974. Showing the wide doorways of the Strachan body and the attractive yellow livery of Tyne & Wear is KGR 536G, originally 136 in the Sunderland fleet. (RS)

Portsmouth Corporation Transport were staunch Leyland buyers; indeed, from 1950 until 1988, when the company was privatised, the only non-Leyland purchases were twelve Swifts delivered in 1969. They lasted until 1981, and pictured on The Hard in Portsmouth shortly after delivery are 179 and 183 (NTP 179/83H). (RC)

The last AECs purchased by Cardiff were twenty Alexander-bodied Swifts delivered in 1968, with seating for forty-seven and space for eighteen standees. They were not a great success, as being underpowered they were prone to overheating. As well as being Cardiff's first buses with a centre exit, and their first high-capacity saloons, they also marked a move away from conductor-operated buses. 517 (MBO 517F) is seen here in a wet Cardiff bus station, wearing the original crimson livery. (AS)

Cardiff again, and still wet. In 1972, a new, more modern image was sought, and a light orange and white livery was chosen. The name City of Cardiff was used in English on one side and in Welsh, Dinas Caerdydd, on the other. Freshly painted MBO 507F is seen in Cardiff bus station in 1973. (AS)

East Kent turned to Alexander to body their final batch of Swifts, and received vehicles similar to London Country's SMA class. Seen shortly after delivery but looking decidedly scruffy around the offside lower panels is YJG 581K. Fitted with AH691 engines, they were reputed to be lively performers, being ideally suited for the hilly terrain around Dover. (AS)

Another fleet created by the 1974 Local Government Reorganisation was Lancaster City Transport, which was formed by the merger of the original Lancaster City Transport with Morecambe & Heysham Corporation. The two fleets had completely different buying policies – Lancaster staying loyal to county manufacturer Leyland, while Morecambe preferred AECs. Seen prior to the merger is Morecambe's number 2 (CTJ 102E), a Strachan-bodied Swift seen in Easton Road, Morecambe, in 1967. (AS)

A batch of nine UTIC U2043 integrals were imported into the UK in 1971 by Moseley, the Loughborough-based dealer. Chassis six was OAG 214L, new to Wood's of Largs; however, in this view taken in Moreton-in-Marsh it had passed to South Wales operator Richard's of Brynmawr. (RS)

The first of the nine was AOH 561K, delivered in 1971 to Bowen's of Birmingham, who, for reasons unknown, only kept it for two months. Surprisingly, Bowen's then purchased a further two second-hand examples in 1974. Seen here in 1976 turning into London's Victoria coach station, and now operated by Rowson of Hayes, it appears to have suffered damage to its offside front corner. (AS)

A UTIC on its home turf. Most of the UTIC/AECs were delivered to RN (Rodoviária Nacional), Portugal's nationalised bus company. Between 1992 and 1995, RN was split into regional operating centres – the first to be sold becoming EVA, looking after operations in the Algarve. Seen at Sagres Harbour on the Sagres–Lagos service is 9700 (AO-92-97). The service was conductor-operated between Sagres and Figueira, the halfway point, where the conductor would alight and meet the bus going back to Sagres. (TW)

Such was the reliability of the UTIC/AEC combination that many were re-bodied for further use. Originally built in 1975 for local service work, by 1993 this AH760-engined example had been fitted with a high-floor Marco Polo coach body. It is seen near the Sabugal depot of operator Viuva Monteiro e Irmao. (MH)

Joao Carlos Soares of Guimaraes operated a large and interesting fleet, which at one time was 50 per cent AEC of varying ages, all renowned for their fitment of whitewall tyres. They were also known for their ability to re-engine vehicles, and counted among their fleet Volvos fitted with AEC engines. Seen here is fleet number 66, the only Volvo-engined AEC. The AECs lasted into this millennium, but their days were numbered when Arriva took over the fleet in 2000. (MH)

Both Arriva and Stagecoach have acquired sizeable operations in Portugal. This short length UTIC belonging to the Stagecoach Portugal operation based around Cascais was powered by an AH760 engine. It was retained by Stagecoach as a spare bus to deputise for a small truck-derived vehicle that worked the tortuous and steep road from Sintra station to the hilltop palace. It is seen at the depot in the company of two unidentified RMA class Routemasters. (MH)

To mark the end of AEC operation with Arriva Portugal, a commemorative running day was held, and PM-47-25, bedecked in a commemorative scheme, stands on the bus station at Póvoa de Varzim. The script on the side is very roughly translated as 'I am the last AEC bus in service with Arriva – I am tired, it is time for me to rest'. (MH)

Formed in 1922 to operate a bus service around Wakefield and Castleford, by the mid-1950s West Riding was the largest bus company in private hands. Well known for their involvement in the ill-fated Guy Wulfrunian project (operating 132 out of the 137 vehicles built), they also favoured AECs. Among the last vehicles purchased before the company was bought by the Transport Holding Company were six Marshall-bodied Swifts; 24 (JHL 824E) is seen at Castleford depot in 1968. (AS)

Being situated between Wolverhampton and Coventry, Birmingham City Transport tended to favour locally built Guy or Daimler products. Only two batches of AECs were purchased – thirteen Regents in 1947 and eighteen Swifts twenty years later. By the time this photo of KOX 665F was taken in 1970, Birmingham had become the largest constituent of the new West Midlands PTE. (AS)

Two vehicles that started their lives in the north-west of England and ended up in the south-east are pictured here in 1990 in the fleet of Auto-Reps of Gravesend. Both operating service 150 from Tunbridge Wells to the Medway Towns, ex-Blackpool Swift OFR 985M, devoid of any identification or route numbering, sits in front of ex-Greater Manchester Atlantean 7553 (HNB 43N). (NG)

Grimsby-Cleethorpes purchased six Swifts in 1967, which were followed two years later by a further three, all bodied by Roe. Although second-hand examples were purchased from Nottingham, no more new Swifts entered the fleet until 1975, when three East Lancs-bodied examples were purchased, including JEE 50P, the last Swift built for the home market. (RS)

BOAC ordered three unusual Sparshatt-bodied Swifts, intended for airside transfer duties at Karachi airport. However, the order was cancelled and they finished their working lives at Heathrow. The buses had half cabs and a platform complete with double jack-knife doors to allow them to manoeuvre right up to aeroplanes on open apron airfields. Despite the order being cancelled early into the build, they were still built to the planned specification with uprated ventilation systems and a sun canopy. C127 (LLH 889K) survives at Brooklands Museum in Surrey. (MH)

In Australia, the Swift was used extensively on long-distance operations and could be fitted with the 12.47 litre AH760 engine. Deanes Coaches of North Ryde, New South Wales, operated seven of these Domino Metroliner 80-bodied Swifts, all delivered in 1980. Seen here under demonstration conditions and advertised as a Leyland Swift, its body sports such desirable features as 'quality vinyl covered seats, round cornered windows and additional rub rail'. (NC)

The Pressed Metal Corporation produced some of the more ornately bodied Swifts for Australia, including AH691-engined MO.4342. Delivered to Hunter Valley Coaches of Maitland, New South Wales, it is seen in 1979 on a Royal Easter Show charter to the Sydney Showground, sporting Leyland badging rather than AEC. (NC)

The original batch of London Transport Merlins were bodied by Strachan, and were considered to be of better build quality than the Metro-Cammell production vehicles. Designed for the Red Arrow concept of high-capacity dual-door standee single-deckers, they entered service in 1966 on route 500 between Victoria and Marble Arch. XMS4 (JLA 4D) is seen approaching Victoria in 1968 in the company of such long-lost names as Midland Bank and Watneys. (AS)

Delivered new in 1970 and withdrawn nine years later after engine failure, SMS162 (EGN 162J) was the sole SMS used as both an official type trainer as well as an Aldenham staff bus, so it probably visited more of London than its stablemates. Seen outside Romford station when new, prominently displayed on its front are the pay as you enter signs, indicating a driver-only vehicle. (AS)

An evocative picture of MBA570 (AML570H) leading two Routemasters across Lambeth Bridge while working Red Arrow Route 507. Originally delivered in 1969 as an MBS-registered VLW507G, it was promptly put into store until January 1970, when it was reconfigured as an MBA. Following withdrawal in 1980, it passed to Harris (Donsway), Faversham, who kept it until 1990 – as long as it had worked for LT. (RC)

The first fifty Swifts had Marshall single door bodies and were intended as RT replacements. Seating forty-two with twenty standees, they were considered equivalent to an RT, which seated fifty-six with five standing. Drivers soon found that the SM's could not go where an RT could, and instant route changes were made. Seen in Hounslow shortly after delivery is SM37 (AML 37H). (AS)

SMS306 (EGN 306J) is seen here newly delivered at Streatham Garage, with RT261 (HLW 248) in the background. It is an indication of how unsuitable the Swifts were with London Transport that despite being nearly twenty-five years older than SMS306, RT261 was only withdrawn a year before it. (AS)

Marshall-bodied SM33 (AML 33H) is seen in Bexleyheath on a 132 working complete with makeshift destination blinds when the route was temporarily covered with SMs. This bus went on to have a long career as routebus 662 in Malta, until it was destroyed by fire in 2010. (AS)

A report published in 1969 identifying the transport needs of Stevenage suggested that a fast and frequent bus network was better than large-scale road building. In 1971, London Transport introduced the Superbus network, initially running from the bus station to Chells using a fleet of Swifts painted in a bright yellow and blue livery. SM486 (DPD 486J) looks resplendent in its new livery, three months after the start of the service. (AS)

The panoramic windows and dual-purpose seating of the SMA class can be seen in this shot of a damp SMA8 (JPF 108K) turning into London Victoria, closely followed by London Country Plaxton-bodied Reliance P5 (SPK 205M). In the background is the former BOAC terminal, now operated by British Airways, with the Park Royal Regal IV half-decks by now replaced by Leyland Atlanteans. (AS)

Above and below: Following the transfer of London Country to the National Bus Company, it became apparent that its fleet age was higher than that of other NBC subsidiaries. Waiting lists for new vehicles were unrealistic, so fellow NBC subsidiary South Wales Transport came to the rescue. Fifteen Willowbrook and Marshall-bodied Swifts – twelve of them only six months old – were transferred to London Country in 1971. Their additional bodyside brightwork set them apart from the Swifts already in residence, as evidenced by SMW13 (XCY 471J), seen in St Albans in 1976. As the vehicles were overhauled, the brightwork was either removed or painted over, and SMW13 is seen again, this time looking rather drab after withdrawal in 1981. (AS top, RC bottom)

Fresh out of the box: on its first day in service in 1971, and seen as direct replacements for RLH class double-deckers, London Country SM479 (DPD 479J) is in Windsor bus station on route 353, heading to Berkhamsted. (AS)

J. H. Wooliscroft of Darley Dale, Derbyshire, traded as Silver Service and operated former MBS569 (AML 569H) until the mid-1980s. Originally put on a school contract, complete with its LT standee interior including turnstile entrance layout it was dubbed 'the cattle truck' by a local newspaper, and following complaints from parents, it was re-seated and moved to alternative work. (RS)

The Malta Education Department took delivery of nearly twenty Swifts for use on school transport, until the whole operation was closed down in 2011. The vehicles were kept in near original condition, resulting in some of the survivors becoming ideal preservation projects, with the rest donating spares for the same. Seen shortly before the end of operations are former SMS259, SM35 and SMS278. (MH)

Exported to Malta in 1981, SMS275 (EGN 275J) was subjected to Maltese-style customisation. While the fitting of flat glass windscreens and a Leyland group Ergomatic cab front grille is aesthetically pleasing, it was underfloor where most of its conversion took place. Gone is the rear-mounted AH505 engine and semi-automatic gearbox, to be replaced with a mid-mounted AV505 and manual box – enough work for its owner to now refer to it as a Reliance. (MH)

Townsend Thoresen purchased three Merlins, including AML 605H, to transfer foot passengers between the terminals and Cross-Channel ferries at Dover docks, where their standee bodies proved ideal for moving large groups of people over short distances. Delivered as MBS605 and registered VLW 605G, it was removed from service after only two months and was recertified as a Red Arrow vehicle, complete with its new identity. Passing through the hands of several more operators after its life on the docks finished, it was scrapped in 1996. (MH)

DPD 478J, formerly SM478, is seen at Gatwick Airport in 1981 with two other vehicles from a batch of five sold for further service while undertaking car park transfer duties. (SG)

The only V8 Sabre bodied for the UK market was CBU 636J, which carried a forty-six-seat ECW body, also to a unique design. First displayed at the 1970 Commercial Motor Show, it was then delivered to Best of Ealing, and entered into the Blackpool Coach Rally the following year. By the time the Sabre was put on the road, AEC was firmly under the British Leyland banner, and there is no indication on the coach at all to show that it was an AEC product. (MH)

By the mid-1970s the Sabre had passed to Kent operator Kemp's Coaches, where it remained for the rest of its operational life, subsequently receiving the cherished number plate SAB 784. By the time this 1979 shot in Hyde Park Corner was taken, a considerable amount of front end restyling had taken place, with new indicators and sidelights and the removal of the large wraparound chrome front. Kemp's later repainted the vehicle and removed all the Leyland badging, replacing them with badges to reflect its true identity by placing the large V8 Sabre badge and an AEC winged triangle across the front. (CE)

The Reliance

Returning to mid-engined chassis, and comparative vehicles to the Regal IV from AEC's competitors were becoming or already were lighter in weight, resulting in that all-important increase in fuel economy. Not wanting to be left behind, AEC developed a medium-weight chassis suitable for both bus and coach operations and built to the new maximum length of 30 feet. Two versions were built; a conventional chassis that was named the Reliance, reviving a name previously used in the 1920s, and an integrally constructed vehicle, built in conjunction with Park Royal and named the Monocoach (oddly named, as records show that the Monocoach was always destined to be a bus rather than a coach). Two demonstration vehicles of each model were completed in 1953: Reliance 135 BMV fitted with a Duple coach body, and Park Royal bus-bodied 50 AMC. Monocoach demonstrators were registered NLP 635 and 210 AMP. NLP 635 was originally sent to work with London Transport; however, as LT had only just finished replacing its fleet of single-deck buses with the Regal IV-based RF, it was not looking for further vehicles of this type.

Originally classed as a medium-weight chassis, the first Reliances were fitted with the 6.75 litre AH410 or 7.75 litre AH470 engine with a variety of gearbox options available, including synchromesh or monocontrol semi-automatic transmission. The first production vehicles entered service in 1954 and were quickly found to be ideally suited for all aspects of passenger operation, whether as a local service bus or a luxury touring coach, and bodybuilders such as Harrington were quick to produce elegant designs to compliment the underfloor-engined chassis layout. The Monocoach, now available with bodies other than Park Royal, initially received some impressive orders, particularly from Northern General, while large orders for Alexander-bodied versions came from various Scottish Bus Group fleets. Sadly, the writing was on the wall for the Monocoach; the claimed weight advantage of the integral construction turned out to be nominal, and it also started to suffer from structural weakness near the spring mountings. By 1957 it had been dropped from the AEC catalogue.

Changes to Construction and Use Regulations saw the maximum length of the Reliance increased twice, firstly in 1961 to 36 feet (11 metres), and finally in 1967 to 40 feet (12 metres). The launch in 1961 of the longer wheelbase chassis with its more powerful AH590 engine came shortly after the first motorways were opened, and many express service operators such as Yelloway of Rochdale and the Alexander Group were quick to see the potential. Later, as the rear-engined layout became more popular for bus use, it was for coaching duties that the bulk of Reliances were sold, and as the bodywork got heavier so the engines got bigger. Firstly to the 11.3 litre AH691, followed by the 12.47 litre AH760, and a 12 metre Reliance, fitted with an AH760, coupled to a six-speed ZF gearbox was seen to be the epitome of British coaching. The last Reliance was built in 1979, former AEC customers being expected to purchase comparative Leyland products – firstly the Leopard, and subsequently the Tiger. Most Leopards were fitted with a semi-automatic gearbox, and such was the reluctance of Reliance operators to buy the semi-automatic Leopard that Leyland offered a ZF manual gearbox as an option for the Leopard. However, it was too little too late, and the continental invasion of DAF, Volvo and Scania had already begun.

Gloucestershire had its fair share of interesting operators, many of which have sadly fallen by the wayside. One operator very much in existence is Marchant's of Cheltenham, who were staunch AEC operators. Kearsey's was an old established name taken over by Marchants in 1968; the Kearsey name and livery remained on their vehicles until withdrawal. Looking rather battle scarred is ex-Kearsey's 76 (ODG 983), a 1955 Burlingham-bodied Reliance. Seen here in 1973 in Cheltenham's Royal Well bus station, it remained in the fleet until 1976. (AS)

Monocoach GWG 472 was new to Walter Alexander & Sons of Falkirk in 1955. In 1961, the Alexander concern was split into three divisions – Fife, Midland and Northern – and AC68 was transferred to the Northern concern, becoming NAC68. Looking every inch a period photograph, it was actually caught on camera well away from home at Staffordshire's Chatterley Whitfield Mining Museum in the early 1990s. (MH)

Buses, trains, bikes and cars all feature in this 1970 shot of Aldershot & District Reliance 555 (MOR 601). Fitted with a Strachan coach body when new in 1955, it was withdrawn in 1967 and re-bodied by MCW. It is seen at Alton station on rail replacement duties (note that both the station hoarding and the windscreen sticker still refer to the company as British Railways). (RC)

The graceful curves of Duple's Britannia body can be seen on 26 HMD. New in 1956 to Gibson of Cockfosters, it passed in 1959 to Silver Service of Darley Dale, where it remained until 1974. Subsequently passing into the hands of travellers, it was last seen in the UK in Blackburn in 1989. In 2007 it was found abandoned in Amsterdam, carrying registration number UTD 295H from an ex-Lancashire United Bristol LH. (MP)

The firm of John. C. Beadle of Dartford, Kent, became known for using components from major chassis manufacturers and building them into their own all-alloy integral vehicles. They also built proprietary bodies, and, being based locally, bodied many vehicles for East Kent, including Reliance MJG 50, seen on layover in Hythe. (RC)

The North Western Road Car Company (NWRCC) operated across Cheshire, Lancashire, Yorkshire, Derbyshire and Staffordshire. In 1969, control of NWRCC passed to the National Bus Company, and in 1972 the company was split, with part of the Cheshire area operations passing to Crosville. Seen at Crosville's Macclesfield depot before the NBC corporate livery came into being is 1956 Willowbrook-bodied Reliance SAA985 (LDB 746). (AS)

The dismantling of North Western in 1972 was triggered by the creation of SELNEC. This 1972 photo of two former North Western Weymann-bodied Reliances taken in Ashton-under-Lyne bus station symbolises the change. LDB724 is still in NWRCC colours while sister vehicle LDB721 has acquired SELNEC (Southern) sunglow orange and cream. (TW)

394 DKK started life in 1958 with Maidstone & District as one of a batch of twenty-four Harrington Wayfarer coach-bodied Reliances. After five years they were looking dated for front line duties, so went back to Harrington, where bus-style fronts complete with destination boxes and jack-knife doors were fitted. They enjoyed a further nine years' service, but by April 1973 394 (and sister 395) had passed to Vagg's of Knockin Heath in Shropshire, lasting only a year before being scrapped. (MP)

The Oxfordshire village of Woodcote was the home of Chiltern Queens, with their splendidly eclectic fleet of AECs. Seen inside the depot are, from left to right: Plaxton Highway-bodied Reliance NBW 407, new to the company in 1958; Weymann-bodied Reliance RCG 618, acquired in 1970 from Aldershot & District; and an ex-Tate & Lyle AEC Mandator tractor unit converted into a breakdown tender. Following the closure of Chiltern Queens, the Mandator was purchased by Staffordshire-based Knotty Bus, the owner of which has contributed many of the pictures in this book. (MP)

In 1959 Grey Cars received six Willowbrook-bodied Reliances, built to a width of 7 feet 6 inches for touring Dartmoor. In 1966, TCR890 (890 ADV) was sold along with sixteen other vehicles to Greenslades of Exeter. It outlived the rest of the batch by some considerable time, and in 1977 was downgraded to a bus, still retaining its coach seating, and transferred to St Austell, staying until 1980, after which it was preserved in Grey Cars livery. (RJ)

W. J. Bence started a bus service in Longwell Green, Bristol, in 1890, diversifying into building bus bodies in 1918. In 1944 the company was renamed Longwell Green Coachworks Ltd, and continued building buses and lorries until 1966. Many of their major customers were from South Wales, including Pontypridd UDC. Under the 1974 Local Government Reorganisation, Pontypridd became Taff-Ely, resulting in 1963 Reliance 997 TTX wearing Pontypridd's dark blue livery, but with Taff-Ely fleetnames. (RS)

East Kent had several buses fitted with roof racks for transporting rowing boats and their teams to regattas across the south coast of England. Eastbourne Sea Regatta in 1975 sees Park Royal-bodied Reliances TFN 435/431 and 424 parked in the coach park, having unloaded their crews. (AS)

Felix Motors was formed in Armthorpe in 1921, the company being named after Felix the Cat, a well-known cartoon character of the time, and for years a cartoon image was used as an emblem on the side of the vehicles. On 1 April 1976, following the retirement of the Managing Director, the company was sold to South Yorkshire PTE, bringing to an end over fifty-five years of operation. Seen at the back of Doncaster depot are two former Felix Reliances – Plaxton Derwent dual-purpose-bodied 1015 (VWT 355F) of 1968 and 1960 Roe-bodied 1012 (9629 WU). (RS)

Formed in 1930 to operate regular express services across South Wales, the chocolate and red livery of Neath & Cardiff Luxury Coaches earned them the nickname 'The Brown Bombers'. In 1953, N&C was sold to the British Electric Traction Company (BET) who aimed to make the fleet 100 per cent AEC – something it achieved in 1967. New in 1959, Park Royal coach-bodied Reliance TWN 558 is seen in Cardiff bus station proudly displaying its N&C motif on the front bulkhead, together with destinations painted along the side. (AS)

Large operator retrenchment leads to opportunity for smaller operators, and such was the case when Bristol Omnibus withdrew the Berkeley to Sharpness service. P. D. & A. C. Stump of Berkeley were quick to step in, purchasing ex-Maidstone & District Weymann-bodied Reliance 291 GKK to operate the service. By 1976, it, together with the rest of the Stump fleet, had passed to the acquisition-hungry Ladvale Group of Dursley, whose fast expansion led to their downfall in the early 1980s. (RS)

In 1961, London Transport bought three experimental one-person-operated Willowbrook-bodied mono control Reliances to possibly replace the RFs. LT was obviously unimpressed as it sold them to Chesterfield Corporation in 1963 and kept the RFs for several more years. 496 ALH, the middle of the three, is seen leaving Vicar Lane in Chesterfield in September 1971. (TW)

New to Western Welsh in 1961, WKG 287 passed to nearby Henley's of Abertillery, where it amassed a remarkable service life, not being withdrawn until the mid-1990s. Henley's kept it in pristine condition, but by the time this picture with its dramatic Welsh background was taken in 1984, it had lost its original AH470 engine, gaining the slightly larger and less problematic AH505. (MH)

A longstanding member of the Berresford Group was Byrne Brothers of Leek, Staffordshire, the business having been purchased by Berresford's in the early 1960s. It continued to operate as an autonomous unit from its original premises, and while Berresford's ivory formed the basis of the livery, a mid-blue colour provided the relief instead of Berresford's Ayres red. Seen in Leek bus station in 1979, Park Royal-bodied Reliance WFN 517 was new to East Kent in 1961. (SG)

A plethora of Reliances operated by Greenslades of Exeter are seen loading for tours in the lower section of Exeter bus station in 1972. 967 HTT, one of nine with Willowbrook Viscount bodies delivered in 1962, is flanked by two unidentified Harrington Grenadiers and three-month-old Plaxton Panorama Elite-bodied RFJ 824H. (AS)

Founded in 1976, Shaftesbury & District provided local bus services across Somerset and Dorset, the opportunities for which arose following service withdrawals by the established operators, Southern National, Western National and Bere Regis. AECs featured heavily over the years, the original vehicle being 967 HTT, from the previous photograph. Also operated was ex-East Kent Park Royal Reliance WFN 513. Seen in a damp and drizzly Yeovil bus station in 1979, its destination blind is set for a location it could well have served with its original owner. (SG)

Peake's of Pontypool can trace their roots back over 130 years, and acquired their first AEC, a seven-month-old ex-works demonstrator, in 1937. Many more were operated over the decades, including 751 LCV, which was one of nine Harrington-bodied Reliances supplied new to Cornish operator Hawkey's of Newquay. It reached Peake's in 1976 when fifteen years old, and is seen here operating a Pontypool local service. (MP)

In 1972 the National Bus Company introduced a corporate livery, which (with one or two notable exceptions) was poppy red or leaf green for buses, and white for coaches. Vehicles capable of fulfilling dual roles had their bottom half painted red or green, with the top half painted white. Seen in Basingstoke in 1974 is Alder Valley 329 (428 DHO) which was new to Aldershot & District in 1961. (AS)

Before transfer to Highland Omnibuses in 1969, the red, green and cream buses of MacBrayne's were a lifeline to communities around the highlands and islands of Scotland. Seen in Inverness in 1971, still in MacBrayne livery but under Highland ownership, is B58 (389 FGB), a 1962 Reliance with Duple Donnington body. The Donnington was a dual-purpose design built at the Duple (Midland) factory in Loughborough, Leicestershire. (AS)

The magnificent Llynfi Valley is the perfect backdrop for an example of possibly the most graceful coach body of the 1960s, Harrington's Cavalier. Llynfi Motors of Maesteg operated a network of bus services around the Maesteg area, and while Leyland was the favoured chassis, several AECs were operated, with 121 NTX coming from Thomas of Port Talbot. Llynfi Motors was sold to the United Welsh Group in 1988, joining South Wales Transport and Brewer of Caerau. (MH)

Formed in the early 1970s, Orpington & District primarily operated between Croydon and the new private housing development at Forestdale. Operating a fleet of elderly buses led to problems, both financially and mechanically, leading to closure in 1981. Two ex-Swindon Willowbrook-bodied Reliances were operated, and 133 CMR is seen here on layover in Croydon on Derby Day in 1976. (SG)

The hilly terrain of the Forest of Dean was a good place to experience the aural effects of hard-working AECs, with the principal operator Edward's of Joys Green operating a fleet of over forty such vehicles. Cantilupe Road in Ross-on-Wye sees Duple Britannia-bodied 510 PYB, new in 1962 to Comfy Lux Coaches (Darch & Wilcox) of Martock. The coach gave over thirteen years' service to Edwards before withdrawal in 1981. (MP)

Alderney, the northernmost of the inhabited Channel Islands, measures just over 3 miles long and 1½ miles wide. Despite its size, it still had a bus company, Riduna Buses, whose fleet was both varied and confusing, as Alderney registration numbers (AY) were reissued when buses were withdrawn. When a batch of narrow Harrington-bodied Reliances from Devon General became available, Riduna purchased four. Seen here in the company of an unidentified member of the fleet are AY 58 (AFJ 79B) – its mainland heritage showing on the destination blind – and AY 750 (AFJ 85B). (RJ)

Thamesdown Transport was the name given to Swindon Corporation under the 1974 Local Government Reorganisation. Swindon operated its first buses in 1907, with ownership remaining in the hands of the Borough Council until 2017. The Swindon fleet was predominantly double-deck, with all but five supplied by Daimler; indeed the only non-Daimler vehicles purchased were eight Leylands and eleven AECs. One of the latter, Willowbrook-bodied 138 (AMR 138B), is seen in typical Swindon weather in 1979. (SG)

In 1978, Roger Brown, owner of Shaftesbury & District, tendered for two Chesterfield Reliances. The tender was accepted and he became the owner of GRA 45C and 497 ALH (one of the three experimental Reliances acquired by Chesterfield from London Transport). GRA 45C was promptly sold to Blue Saloon of Guildford to supplement the RT fleet. It is seen shortly after acquisition in Guildford, showing Blue Saloon's comprehensive destination blind to good effect. (MH)

In order to negotiate the narrow streets, tight bends and abrupt gradient changes around Halifax, the Joint Committee purchased ten Albion Nimbuses in 1963. Woefully underpowered, they were sold in 1967 and replaced with seven Reliances, which were fitted with special short, narrow bodies built by Pennine Coachcraft. Seen in Bradford in 1971 shortly after Halifax merged with Todmorden to form Calderdale Joint Omnibus Committee is 255 (ECP 955D). (AS)

South Wales again, with the sadly long-gone Edmunds of Rassau, a traditional independent in every sense. Two recently acquired Bristol REs, still in NBC livery, keep company with two Reliances and a Leyland Leopard. The Plaxton Panorama Elite Express-bodied Reliance on the right was JWO 891L, which was purchased new, and went on to further service with Knotty Bus. Willowbrook-bodied CAX 19K was also bought new. The Bristols came from Bristol itself, while the Leopard came the short distance from Merthyr Corporation. (MH)

Another acquisition by the Berresford Group was the three-vehicle fleet of the elaborately named Brown's Direct Coal & Haulage, trading as Mosswood Tours. Plaxton Panorama-bodied Reliance HAR 215C was reportedly not for the faint hearted due to its AEC constant mesh gearbox. (MH)

If the beige destination blinds weren't clue enough, the centre entrances on this pair of Plaxton Panorama-bodied Reliances indicate they were new to Glenton Tours of London. Glenton specified centre entrances and a maximum of thirty-eight seats, with each double seat staggered so that passengers had an uninterrupted view out of the window opposite. No fleet numbers were carried, as registration numbers rose consecutively with each new coach. By 1975, 103 and 108 had passed to Sydenham Coaches, and are pictured with their chrome gleaming in Eastbourne coach park. (AS)

The buses of Taff-Ely District Council passed to Taff-Ely Transport Ltd – a new company set up under the 1985 Transport Act to assume control of the former municipal fleet. The last Reliance operated by the original fleet was Willowbrook-bodied 9 (GTG 91L), new in 1972 and which lasted until the end of operations in 1986. Seen in Pontypridd in 1980, its traditional-looking body contrasting with the Metro-Scania to the left and Leyland National to the right, yet all three were new over the same two-year period. (MH)

The Plaxton Panorama body fitted to Starr of North Anston's 1971 Reliance JWT 743J had been superseded by the Panorama Elite several years earlier. The founder of Starr's disliked the Elite, so had JWT 743J built as a special order. The coach took twelve months to build as the chassis had been delivered to the factory with a set-back front axle to accommodate grant doors and the planned body had already been assembled. After completion, it attended the Blackpool Coach Rally, where, much to Plaxton's embarrassment, it gained more order enquiries than the Elite. (RS)

BAN 115H was new to Glenton in 1970 and is seen when brand new picking up on Eccleston Bridge, London, at the start of a 'Tour of Britain'. No bright colours, no garish fleet livery, yet the little Plaxton Panorama Elite-bodied Reliance just oozes refinement and class, topped off by the smartly uniformed driver. (AS)

Seen on the seafront at Pavoa de Varzim is what must have ranked as one of the oldest buses acquired by Arriva during their first Portuguese buying spree. The 505-engined Reliance/UTIC, its steel body showing signs of corrosion, hadn't long left to go in service, just making it into the current millennium, by which time it was more than thirty years old. (MH)

This Portuguese UTIC-bodied Reliance service bus from the fleet of Viacao Costa & Lino had been spruced up for the celebratory event to mark the end of Arriva Portugal's AEC operation. The VCL fleet had become part of the Joao Carlos Soares (JCS) empire, receiving that company's colours and characteristic white-walled tyres. Along with the largely AEC fleets of Abilio de Costa and Ami Transportes, the JCS fleet became the first purchases of Arriva in Portugal. It is credit to their owners that so many survived for so long in often punishing conditions. Dual entrance-bodied 145 (GP-80-07) is seen here in Famalicao bus station in February 2005. (MH)

I make no apologies for including one modern-day photograph when it is of such an important vehicle. OTG 44R was the very last AH505-engined 'middleweight' Reliance built, and is fitted with a forty-five-seat 10-metre Duple Dominant body. Registered new to Wenellt Coaches (Crooke) of Cardiff, its AEC constant mesh gearbox proved unpopular and in 1980 it passed to Mid-Devon Coaches of Bow. Always earmarked for preservation, upon withdrawal it was acquired by the late Phil Platt, and is seen in Wellington, Somerset, in 2014, looking as good as new. (MH)

The red and cream vehicles of Barton of Chilwell were a familiar sight across the East Midlands, with both double- and single-deck AECs operated. Most vehicles were bought new, but second-hand purchases were made, including Willowbrook-bodied Reliance 1129 (FUP 272C). Seen in Nottingham's Broad Marsh bus station with Weekday Cross signal box in the background, it was bought from Stanhope Motor Services, whose colours were similar enough to Barton's for them to run it 'as acquired'. (RC)

AEC were quick to make the Reliance capable of being bodied to the new maximum length of 36 feet when legislation was changed in 1961. The immaculate fleet of Surrey Motors, Sutton, operated nearly fifty AECs during their existence, including three 36-foot Harrington-bodied examples new in 1965. By the time this picture was taken in Cambridge's Drummer Street bus station ten years later, HLP 10C, along with sister vehicle HLP 11C, had passed to Premier Travel. (AS)

Shortly after the end of the First World War, Alfred Smith bought an ex-Army lorry. His mother-in-law suggested fitting it with a charabanc body, and from these humble beginnings Smith's Luxury Coaches of Reading grew to be one of Southern England's largest coach companies. Smith's purchased their first new Reliance in 1954, and over the next twenty-two years purchased over thirty more. The first 11-metre examples were a pair with Duple Commander III bodies, purchased in 1968, with LRD 858F seen in Eastbourne in 1970. Following the death of Alfred Smith, control of the company passed to Armchair of Brentford. (AS)

John Abbott & Sons of Blackpool operated a large fleet of Reliances, not only across an extensive day excursion programme, as can be seen from the advertising posters next to Plaxton-bodied RFV 897H, but also a regular service between the Fylde coast and Manchester. Abbott's always specified the number seven as the last number on the registration plate of vehicles bought new. (RJ)

Above, below and opposite below: A wonderful story to evidence the strength and reliability of the Reliance involves Plaxton Panorama Elite WBU 670H. Supplied new in 1970 to Ivory Coaches of Tetbury, the Oldham registration explained by the supplying dealer Lancashire Motor Traders having a controlling interest in Ivory Coaches. The Ivory business was sold to the Ladvale Group in 1975, WBU being included even though it had been involved in a serious accident a few weeks earlier. The chassis was deemed to be in excellent shape, so was sent to Plaxton's and emerged in December 1976 as PUJ 54R, fitted with a brand new twenty-eight-seat full executive Plaxton Supreme body. In 1979 it was sold to Young's Coaches of Rampton, Cambridgeshire, who carried out a major rebuild of the coach, including replacing the AH691 engine with a Bedford 500 unit. The extent of the rebuild was sufficient enough to warrant a new identity and in April 1980 it entered service with Young's, registered DER 112V. It still retained its executive interior, complete with television and toilet – fitments taken for granted in coaches nowadays, but still something of a rarity nearly forty years ago. (MP)

Introduced into the UK market in 1969, Portuguese-built Caetano bodywork (marketed through the Moseley dealership in Loughborough) rapidly established itself onto the British coaching scene, with forty-four Caetano Lisboa-bodied Reliances delivered over the following seven years. An early advocate of these bodies was Ron Bonas (Supreme Coaches) of Coventry, who took delivery of three in 1970. SVC 702H left Coventry in 1974 for a new home on the North Wales coast with Pye's of Colwyn Bay, where it went on to do another eight years' work. (MP)

In 1973 Caetano updated the Lisboa, the most obvious amendments being the front-end styling with the head and fog lights lowered, slightly less chrome around the grille area and removal of the Lisboa name. After the initial interest shown in the Caetano range, orders tailed off, and after RVT 577M had been delivered to Procter of Stoke-on-Trent, only three more Lisboas were delivered, marking the end of Caetano-bodied Reliances. (RS)

Alexander of Falkirk introduced the Y Type in 1962, which had a twenty-one-year production life, appearing in bus, dual-purpose and full coach versions. Scottish Bus Group fleets received over 85 per cent of Y Type production, but large batches were delivered to operators south of the border. The dominant operator in North Staffordshire was Stoke-based PMT (Potteries Motor Traction), who took delivery of twenty-five over five years. 170 (FEH 170J) was one of the last, and is seen when brand new displaying PMT's red and cream livery to good effect on a bowls tour to Eastbourne in 1971. (AS)

Seen in Dorchester in 1972 while operating a National Travel duplicate service to Cheltenham is Bere Regis' brand new Duple Viceroy-bodied RJT 681K. This was one of eight coaches bought in April of that year, five of which were Reliances. One wonders how disappointed the young lady on the right would be if she knew she wasn't the focus of the picture. (AS)

Arlington's were quick to follow Moseley's lead by importing Belgian-built Van Hool coachwork. Six 'Vistadome'-bodied Reliances were built, the most opulent of which was VUR 227K. It was supplied to Best of Ealing as a twenty-eight-seat full executive, winning Coach of the Year at the 1972 Brighton Coach Rally. In later life it moved to Layston Coaches in Hertfordshire, whose owner converted it into a motor caravan, and it remains active in this role at the time of writing. (AS)

East Kent were keen to re-body time-expired vehicles with coachwork of a more modern appearance. In 1972–73, two batches of Park Royal-bodied Reliances were sent to Plaxton, receiving Panorama Elite bodies. All retained their 'FN' registrations, the first batch being 519–538FN in 1972, followed by 6539–6548FN a year later. After a further ten years' service with East Kent, at least fifteen of them passed to Caroline Seagull of Great Yarmouth, where 6539 FN from the 1973 batch is seen loading on the seafront for an evening tour. (MH)

Willowbrook had been under the control of Duple since 1958, regaining independence in 1971. Duple restricted Willowbrook to only building bus bodies, but now free of restriction, Willowbrook re-entered the coach market. Their first offering was the 002 Expressway, which was more dual-purpose than full coach. While the large side windows were passenger friendly, their size combined with the thin body pillars led to relatively short lives due to rotting and breaking. XRA 876L was delivered to Silver Service of Darley Dale in 1972. (RS)

By the early 1970s, London Country was looking to replace the time-expired RF class, and took delivery of the ninety-strong RP class Reliances fitted with dual-purpose Park Royal bodies, with single-deck versions of the body on the double-deck AN class of Leyland Atlantean. Fitted with folding doors, coach-style seats, and in some cases a full boot, they remained in service until 1984. The last operational vehicle was RP25 (JPA 125K), which is seen picking up in Buckingham Palace Road, announcing its last in class status via a headboard in the windscreen. (RJ)

With a Trans-Pennine DMU creeping into the background, the clean lines of the Duple Viceroy are shown in this photo of NWY 333K, delivered new to Billie's of Bridlington in 1971. To its right is a Seddon Pennine-bodied Viceroy, the upright engine of which necessitated a higher body profile, which is clearly seen when comparing the waist rails of the two coaches. (RS)

Duple's Dominant body was introduced at the 1972 Commercial Motor Show, with East Kent going on to be the largest operator of Dominant-bodied Reliances. By the time this photograph was taken, Green Line had increased their National Express commitment and required extra vehicles. D17 (PFN 794M) coming via National Travel (South East) is seen departing London Victoria en route to Birmingham. (RC)

Following the inroads made by Van Hool and Caetano, a third continental body builder attempted to crack the UK market. Belgian company Jonckheere imported a handful of bodies in the early 1970s, including two Solaire-bodied Reliances – 11-metre NAC 276L, and 12-metre HKO 349L. New to Whitworth of Ashford, after just five months it was purchased by The King's Ferry. It later passed to Harris of Bromsgrove, where it is seen crossing the seafront at Weston-super-Mare. Its last owner was Spearing's of Willand, Devon, where it was scrapped in the early 1990s. (RS)

Once a familiar sight on the roads of the UK and Europe, Smiths Happiway-Spencer was the trading name of the Wigan-based Blundell Group, one of the constituent parts of what is now Shearings Holidays. The first AECs entered the group in 1949, and the marque remained part of the fleet until the last Reliances were delivered in 1980. One of the first Dominants bought was 9 (MED 407P), seen at Wembley in 1978 for the Leeds *v*. St Helens Challenge Cup Final. No doubt St Helens blamed their 14–12 loss on travelling on a coach from Wigan! (AS)

I have managed to get this far without including a picture of that doyen of AEC operators, Yelloway of Rochdale. Up until their purchase by the ATL group in 1985, Yelloway only bought British-built vehicles, the vast majority of which were AECs. Altogether nearly 150 AECs were owned, including the first 12-metre examples delivered to a British operator. Every season saw new vehicles delivered to operate Yelloway's network of express coach services, yet only two Reliances were ever bodied by Duple – NNC 850/5P, and the shorter of the two was NNC 850P, which is seen here in Bristol docks operating the South West Clipper. (AS)

Not many NBC subsidiaries operated AEC coaches, the products of Leyland and Bristol being the preferred options. National Travel (South West) purchased eleven semi-automatic Dominant-bodied examples in 1976, which were then split between the Wessex of Bristol and Black & White of Cheltenham operating units. Seen here in London Victoria is 155 (NDF 155P), which went on to be the last Reliance coach operated by the NBC, being retained for use on the Wessex Airlink service between Bristol and Bristol Airport. (AS)

The immaculately presented chocolate and yellow vehicles of Surrey Motors of Sutton were a familiar sight until 1980, when the decision was made by the company to cease coaching operations. It is fitting, therefore, that not only were AECs the first new vehicles delivered to the company, but the Reliances delivered in 1979 were the last. Fitted with a late Plaxton Panorama Elite body, LGH 432P is seen at the Devil's Punchbowl, Hindhead, in 1979 (SG)

The mainstay of Yelloway's fleet in the 1970s were Plaxton Supreme-bodied Reliances, with six vehicles entering service every year that the combination was available. All front line coaches were fitted with luxurious Chapman reclining seats, and when new coaches entered the fleet their seats were put into store, to be replaced by the Chapmans from the coaches they were replacing. Looking uncharacteristically down-at-heel with blackened rear wheel and no AEC winged triangle is NNC 852P, which is seen in the company of sister ship SBU 304R. (RJ)

Looking every inch like one of the continental invasion, OYT 530R was one of four Willowbrook 007-bodied Reliances built for National Travel (South East). NT (SE) required left-hand drive coaches to undertake Europabus services, and as Willowbrook already had type approval to build LHD bodies suitable for fitting to the Reliance due to a contract to supply similar vehicles to the MoD, it was quicker than waiting for Plaxton or Duple to gain the same accreditation. They were the last British-built vehicles to be fitted with roof-mounted luggage racks, which are just visible here on OYT 530R, seen stood on Maderia Drive, Brighton, at the 1977 British Coach Rally. (AS)

The Duchy of Cornwall welcomes huge numbers of visitors every year, but their travel requirements are vastly different to those of forty years ago, the increase in car ownership seeing the decline of the traditional day trips by coach, and with it the loss of some old, established operators. The village of Tintagel, closely associated with the legend of King Arthur, was also the home of Fry's Coaches until closure in 1998, who were well known for their Harrington-bodied Reliances, most of which came from the Devon General group. Only one Reliance was bought new – Plaxton Supreme-bodied PAF 315R, which is seen here in Falmouth in 1982. (MH)

Prior to branching out into bus operation, keen Reliance users Armchair of Brentford were big players in the London tourist market. Usually Plaxton coachwork was specified; however, the last two purchased in 1979 were fitted with Van Hool Aragon bodies. Tourists can be quite demanding when it comes to the coaches they travel on, and Armchair's coaches were well-appointed, most vehicles having a reduced seating capacity to allow for extra leg room and reclining seats trimmed in a bright red colour to match the fleet livery. WRO 438S is seen outside the Forum Hotel in London, with Trathen's MAN SR280 ADV 154Y parked behind. (RJ)

One of the first operators to order 36-foot Reliances was Premier Travel, ordering two Alexander-bodied examples in 1964. They continued buying this chassis and bodywork combination for every new purchase until 1974, when the first Plaxtons arrived into the fleet. One of the last was 245 (OJE 551N), which, despite being new in 1974, was fitted with an AEC metal instrument binnacle rather than a moulded dashboard. It is seen at the company's Haverhill depot in the company of Plaxton Supreme-bodied 259 (NEB 346R) and 261 (NEB 348R), showing Premier's unusual three panel destination display – a feature for many years on all coaches that were bought new. (SG)

All but one of Duple's Dominant bus-bodied Reliances were delivered to Scottish operators, with Hutchison of Overtown purchasing eleven. MacConnacher (Gaelicbus) of Ballachulish subsequently acquired seven of the eleven, including ESU 423T. Gaelicbus began competing with Highland Scottish Omnibuses in the Fort William area in the mid-1980s – one of the more unlikely settings for competitive action – but succumbed to the inevitable and in the summer of 1996 sold out to Highland, which was by then part of the Rapson Group. (RJ)

The Reliance, usually fitted with ZF six-speed gearbox, was also Hutchison's vehicle of choice for its front-line coaching fleet. Parked in Inveraray, overlooking the upper reaches of Loch Fyne with the towers of Inveraray Castle just visible behind the driver's head, is Plaxton Supreme-bodied GSU 7T, looking every inch an AEC with its gleaming winged triangle and chrome nut guard rings. (MH)

Premier Travel again, and one from the last batch of Reliances purchased before the closure of Southall. WEB406 – 11T were all fitted with six-speed manual gearboxes, but while 406 and 407 had Plaxton Supreme III bodies, the remainder of the batch were fitted with Supreme IVs. 278 (WEB 408T) is seen turning onto Emmanuel Street, Cambridge, having just worked in on service 39, the 'Varsity Express', which linked Cambridge and Oxford and was operated jointly with Percival's coaches of Oxford. (MH)

The Gloucester village of Winchcombe was home to the smart black-liveried fleet of Castleways Coaches. With no specific vehicle-buying policy, additions to the fleet were whatever took the eye of Trevor Fogarty when he was on the lookout for new vehicles. Only two AECs were operated from new – BAD 549/50T, both of which were fitted with Duple Dominant II bodies, and the latter of the pair is seen powering away from the depot in 1983. (MH)

Above and below: The London Country RS and RB class were an overdue attempt to halt the decline in Green Line patronage, previous modernisation attempts being less than successful due to the unreliability of the earlier RC and RP classes. The LNC and SNC (Leyland National) classes brought reliability, but with plastic seats, engine noise and lack of first-class amenities that Green Line customers paid for. In 1977, the first Green Line vehicles that had recognisable coach bodies arrived: the Duple Dominant-bodied RB class (Reliance Blackpool, the home of Duple), and Plaxton Supreme RS class (Reliance Scarborough, the home of Plaxton). All were 11 metres long, and were acquired on a five-year lease from Kirby Central. By 1981 the leases started to expire, and the coaches had to be returned to the lessors in (or as near as practicable) the condition they were received in, so were sent for refurbishment, many going to Midland Red or United Counties at Milton Keynes. By the end of 1985 they had all gone, and operators were quick to snap up the refurbished coaches. One of each class is pictured in central London – Duple-bodied RB122 (EPM 122V) and Plaxton-bodied RS140 (EPM 140V). (RJ)

The last Reliance built with a Duple Dominant bus body, and the only one not delivered to a Scottish operator, was JTM 109V. New to Tillingbourne of Cranleigh, it passed to their sister company Metrobus before passing to London & Country for use on school work – a rather unusual vehicle to appear in the fleet of a major operator. It is now preserved by one of the original directors of Metrobus, but is seen here waiting time in Guildford bus station in 1980. (SG)

The majority of the last Reliances were cancelled chassis from the Greenline RB and RS order, and were fitted with floor-mounted pedestal-controlled semi-automatic gearboxes. Snell's Coaches of Newton Abbot bought three of the last, including two with X registrations. WOD 225X, being the last of the three, is seen here in Southsea in 1985. At the same time, Snell's re-bodied two Reliances with narrow Duple Dominant coach bodies, with at least one later receiving a Scania engine, its performance becoming legendary among drivers in the South West. (RJ)

The only Y plate Reliance was ACX 785Y, delivered to Abbeyways–Ivesways as TVH 138X, and was one of two (the other being TVH 134X) that were fitted from new with the deeper Viewmaster screen. It was never used with its original number, the owner wanting to have the distinction of putting the last new registered AEC on the road. By 1991 it had passed to Gordon's of Rotherham. (RS)

While ACX 785Y was the last *new* Reliance registered, it was not the last to be registered. When East Kent needed to upgrade their National Holidays fleet in 1983, they took the surprise step to re-body ten 1973 Duple Dominant-bodied Reliances with Berkhof 'Esprit' bodies. The chassis were allocated new 'EBC' chassis numbers by Ensign, who also undertook power steering conversions, allowing the allocation of new registrations rather than keeping their original plates as the previous East Kent rebodies had. The Berkhof bodies must have been well built, for some stayed in service until 2009. A198 TAR gives an idea how the Reliance would have looked had it not been discontinued. (RS)